What's the Issue?

WHO ARE IMMIGRANTS?

By Riley Lawrence

KidHaven PUBLISHING

Published in 2019 by
KidHaven Publishing, an Imprint of Greenhaven Publishing, LLC
353 3rd Avenue
Suite 255
New York, NY 10010

Designer: Andrea Davison-Bartolotta
Editor: Katie Kawa

Photo credits: Cover (top) Ryan Rodrick Beiler/Shutterstock.com; cover (bottom) Riccardo Piccinini/Shutterstock.com; p. 4 Torgado/Shutterstock.com; p. 5 Spencer Platt/Getty Images; p. 7 (main) Drew Angerer/Getty Images; p. 7 (inset) courtesy of National Park Service; p. 8 Oscity/Shutterstock.com; p. 9 Fotosearch/Getty Images; p. 11 RHONA WISE/AFP/Getty Images; p. 12 Sk Hasan Ali/Shutterstock.com; p. 13 XiXinXing/Shutterstock.com; p. 15 STILLFX/Shutterstock.com; p. 17 John Gomez/Shutterstock.com; p. 19 (bottom) Chip Somodevilla/Getty Images; p. 19 (top) Karla Ann Cote/NurPhoto via Getty Images; p. 20 Rawpixel.com/Shutterstock.com; p. 21 Apostrophe/Shutterstock.com.

Library of Congress Cataloging-in-Publication Data

Names: Lawrence, Riley, 1993- author.
Title: Who are immigrants? / Riley Lawrence.
Description: New York : KidHaven Publishing, 2019. | Series: What's the
  issue? | Includes index.
Identifiers: LCCN 2017058449| ISBN 9781534525795 (library bound book) | ISBN
  9781534525801 (pbk. book) | ISBN 9781534525818 (6 pack) | ISBN 9781534525825 (ebook)
Subjects: LCSH: United States–Emigration and immigration–Juvenile
  literature. | Immigrants–United States–Juvenile literature.
Classification: LCC JV6450 .L38 2019 | DDC 305.9/06912–dc23
LC record available at https://lccn.loc.gov/2017058449

Printed in the United States of America

CPSIA compliance information: Batch #BS18KL: For further information contact Greenhaven Publishing LLC, New York, New York at 1-844-317-7404.

Please visit our website, www.greenhavenpublishing.com. For a free color catalog of all our high-quality books, call toll free 1-844-317-7404 or fax 1-844-317-7405.

CONTENTS

On the Move

Most people move at some point during their lives. They might move to a new neighborhood, a new city, or even a new state. Some people travel even farther and move to a new country. These people are known as immigrants.

Throughout history, millions of immigrants have come to the United States. They're often looking to build a better life for themselves and their families. However, some people aren't kind to immigrants, and this can make life in a new country hard. Read on to learn more about immigrants and the ways you can help make them feel at home!

Facing the Facts 🔍

As of 2015, more than 43 million people living in the United States were born in a **foreign** country.

AMERICA'S GOT ROOM IMMIGRANTS WELCOME

No importa de dónde eres, estamos contentos que seas nuestro vecino.

No matter where you are from, we're glad you're our neighbor.

لا يهم اين ولدتم، و
لكننا سعداء انتم
جيراننا.

Although some people are afraid of immigrants, most people believe immigrants should be welcomed.

Coming to America

The United States is often called a nation of immigrants. That's because the people who live there were either born somewhere else themselves or are **descendants** of people who were born somewhere else. Most scientists and historians believe that even Native Americans are descendants of people who first came to what's now the United States from Asia.

However, not everyone who came to the United States wanted to move there. Until the 1800s, people were brought from Africa as slaves. Unlike immigrants, slaves had no choice but to leave their homes. They worked in the United States for no pay and were treated as property.

Facing the Facts

Many people believe the first settlers to come to North America crossed a piece of land known as the Bering Land Bridge, or Beringia, which connected present-day Siberia and Alaska.

Immigrants have helped make the United States a more diverse country, which means it's made up of many different kinds of people.

Bering Land Bridge

Arctic Ocean

SIBERIA

NORTHEAST RUSSIA

CHUKCHI SEA

ALASKA
USA

Lena River

Kolyma River

Chukotka Pen.

Seward Pen.

Yukon River

Mackenzie River

CANADA

BERING SEA

Kamchatka Pen.

Alaska Pen.

Gulf of Alaska

Pacific Ocean

0   250   500
miles

USA

WE ARE ALL IMMIGRANTS

Early Immigrants

After the United States became an independent country, the first immigrants to come to the new nation were generally from Great Britain and other parts of western and northern Europe. Irish immigrants began coming to the United States in large numbers after the Great **Famine**, which began in 1845.

During the late 1800s and early 1900s, immigrants began to come from eastern Europe, southern Europe, and Asia. The **Industrial Revolution** created new jobs in the United States, and immigrants saw it as a land of opportunity. Between 1880 and 1930, more than 27 million immigrants came to the United States.

Ellis Island

8

Facing the Facts

Many immigrants entered the United States through Ellis Island in New York. Today, visitors to Ellis Island can walk through an immigration museum.

Many people living in the United States today are descendants of immigrants who came to the country more than 100 years ago. Learning about your family history can be a good way to learn more about the history of immigration.

Changes in Immigration

For many years, most immigrants to the United States came from Europe. However, that's no longer the case. Today, most immigrants come from Asia, Africa, and Latin America.

This shift is mainly because of amendments, or changes, made to the Immigration and Nationality Act in 1965. These changes ended old systems of quotas, or numbers of people allowed into the United States, that were based on the countries immigrants were coming from. The amendments gave people from countries outside Europe a more equal chance of being able to live in the United States.

Facing the Facts 🔍

As of 2017, no more than 7 percent of the total number of immigrants to the United States can come from one country. This is done to make the immigrant population more balanced.

IMMIGRATION FORMS

People who want to come to the United States generally must apply for a visa first. A visa is a document that allows a person to seek entry into the United States for different reasons, including immigration.

7880B

FOM POU IMIGRASYON SELMAN
SOLAMENTE PLANILLA DE INMIGRACION

Why Do They Come?

Immigrants have many different reasons for moving to a new country. Finding work has driven people to migrate, or move, to new places for centuries. The United States is seen by many as a place to go to find better-paying jobs or to get the kind of education that can lead to a better job.

Family ties play a big part in immigration, too. People often move to a new country to be closer to members of their family or to build a better life for their loved ones.

Facing the Facts 🔍

A refugee is a person who has to move to a new country. Refugees have a good reason to believe they'd die if they stayed in their home country.

Some immigrants run their own businesses. Supporting these businesses is a good way to help immigrants in your community.

From Green Card to Citizenship

Immigrating to the United States isn't easy. In order to officially and **permanently** live and work in the United States, a person needs a permanent resident card, which is commonly known as a green card. They can get this card because of their job, by marrying a U.S. citizen, or because they're a refugee, among other reasons.

Getting a green card is the first step an immigrant can take toward becoming a U.S. citizen, which grants them certain rights, including the right to vote. This **process** is called naturalization.

Facing the Facts 🔍

As of 2017, up to 50,000 green cards are available each year through the Diversity Immigrant Visa Program. The people who are given these green cards are chosen at **random** from a group that can only include people from countries with low numbers of immigrants to the United States.

Naturalization Test Questions

- **What is the name of the President of the United States now?**

- **What do we show loyalty to when we say the Pledge of Allegiance?**

- **Who is the "Father of Our Country"?**

- **What is the capital of the United States?**

- **When do we celebrate Independence Day?**

These are just some of the questions immigrants may be asked on their naturalization test. In addition to passing this test, there are other requirements for becoming a U.S. citizen, including being at least 18 years old, having a green card for at least 5 years, and taking an **oath** of citizenship.

15

Undocumented Immigrants

Although many immigrants in the United States live there with proper documents, such as green cards, some don't. These immigrants are known as undocumented or unauthorized immigrants, and they're often only granted **temporary** visas but choose not to leave when they're supposed to. In other cases, they sneak into the United States. People sometimes call undocumented immigrants "illegal immigrants," but many believe that's a hurtful term.

Some U.S. citizens want to send all undocumented immigrants back to the countries they came from. This is called deportation.

Facing the Facts 🔍

President Barack Obama started the Deferred Action for Childhood Arrivals (DACA) program to help young undocumented immigrants. These young people, called Dreamers, were **protected** from deportation and were able to work and go to college in the United States. In 2017, President Donald Trump's **administration** announced plans to possibly end DACA unless Congress saved it.

17

How Are Immigrants Treated?

Immigration is at the center of many **debates** in the United States. Some people are afraid that immigration hurts U.S. workers because there are more people looking for jobs. Other people worry that some immigrants might come to the United States to hurt U.S. citizens.

President Trump has said he wants to build a wall to keep undocumented Mexican immigrants out of the United States. He also signed a ban on travel and immigration from countries he believes are a danger to the United States. Some Americans think these **policies** will keep them safe, while others feel they're unfair.

Facing the Facts

According to a 2016 study, Americans are less worried than they were 10 years ago about immigrants taking their jobs.

Different groups of people have different points of view about immigration. This plays a part in how immigrants are treated.

Ways to Be Welcoming

It's not always easy for immigrants to get used to life in a new country. They often have to learn a new language and a new way of life. Sometimes, they even face people who don't like them just because they come from a different country.

There are many things you can do to help immigrants feel welcome in your community. Listening to them and learning about their way of life is a great place to start. Immigrants work hard to make a new home for themselves and their families, and it's easy to help them!

Facing the Facts 🔍

As of 2015, the majority of Americans believe immigrants make the United States a stronger country.

WHAT CAN YOU DO?

Welcome immigrants in your school or community.

Support businesses in your community run by immigrants.

Learn more about immigration issues.

Raise money for groups that help immigrants.

Remind others to treat immigrants with respect and not use hurtful terms such as "illegal immigrants."

Talk to immigrants, and learn about their lives.

Write to government leaders about protecting and helping immigrants.

Helping immigrants might seem like a big job, but these are just some of the ways you can get started. Even the smallest act of kindness can help an immigrant feel welcome!

GLOSSARY

administration: A group of people who manage something, such as a government.

debate: An argument or discussion about an issue, generally between two sides. Also, to take part in such an argument or discussion.

descendant: Someone related to a person or group of people who lived at an earlier time.

famine: A problem in which many people do not have enough to eat.

foreign: Located outside a place or country.

Industrial Revolution: An era of social and economic change marked by advances in technology and science.

oath: A formal and serious promise to tell the truth or do something.

permanently: Lasting for a very long time or forever.

policy: A set of guidelines or rules that set up a course of action.

process: A series of actions that lead to a certain result.

protect: To keep safe.

random: Lacking a clear pattern.

temporary: Lasting for a short amount of time.

FOR MORE INFORMATION

WEBSITES

Meet Young Immigrants

teacher.scholastic.com/activities/immigration/young_immigrants/

Visitors to this website can read stories and watch videos of real children who have recently immigrated to the United States.

A Timeline of Ellis Island

www.libertyellisfoundation.org/ellis-timeline

This website features a timeline of major moments in the history of immigration to the United States.

BOOKS

Baker, Brynn. *Life in America: Comparing Immigrant Experiences.* North Mankato, MN: Capstone Press, 2016.

Howell, Sara. *Undocumented Immigrants.* New York, NY: PowerKids Press, 2015.

Poole, H. W. *Immigrant Families.* Broomall, PA: Mason Crest, 2017.

INDEX